Charles Gounod, John Henry Cornell

Mass of the Sacred Heart of Jesus for Chorus and Orchestra

Charles Gounod, John Henry Cornell

Mass of the Sacred Heart of Jesus for Chorus and Orchestra

ISBN/EAN: 9783337350888

Printed in Europe, USA, Canada, Australia, Japan

Cover: Foto ©Lupo / pixelio.de

More available books at **www.hansebooks.com**

Mass

of the

Sacred Heart of Jesus

for

Chorus and Orchestra

by

CH? GOUNOD.

Revised by J. H. Cornell.

New-York, G. Schirmer.

35 Union Square.

3214.

MESSE DU SACRÉ CŒUR DE JÉSUS.

MASS OF THE SACRED HEART OF JESUS.

Nº 1. KYRIE.

CH. GOUNOD.

4

№ 2. GLORIA.

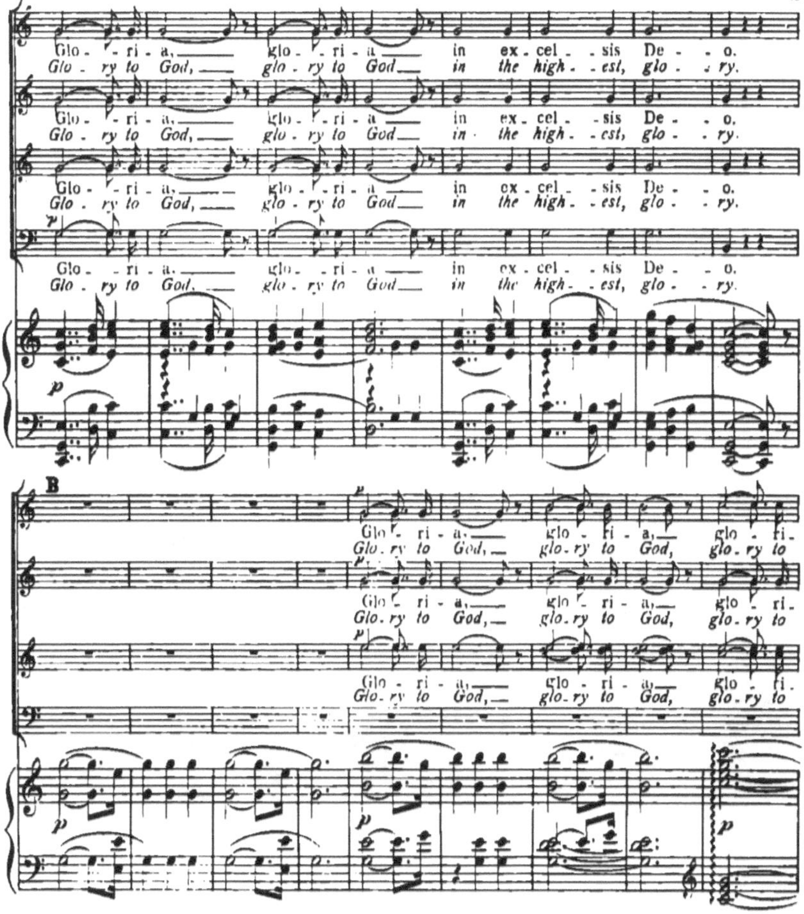
Glo - ri - a, glo - ri - a in ex - cel - sis De - o.
Glo - ry to God, glo - ry to God in the high - est, glo - ry.
Glo - ri - a, glo - ri - a in ex - cel - sis De - o.
Glo - ry to God, glo - ry to God in the high - est, glo - ry.
Glo - ri - a, glo - ri - a in ex - cel - sis De - o.
Glo - ry to God, glo - ry to God in the high - est, glo - ry.
Glo - ri - a, glo - ri - a in ex - cel - sis De - o.
Glo - ry to God, glo - ry to God in the high - est, glo - ry.
B
Glo - ri - a, glo - ri - a, glo - ri
Glo - ry to God, glo - ry to God, glo - ry to
Glo - ri - a, glo - ri - a, glo - ri
Glo - ry to God, glo - ry to God, glo - ry to
Glo - ri - a, glo - ri - a, glo - ri
Glo - ry to God, glo - ry to God, glo - ry to

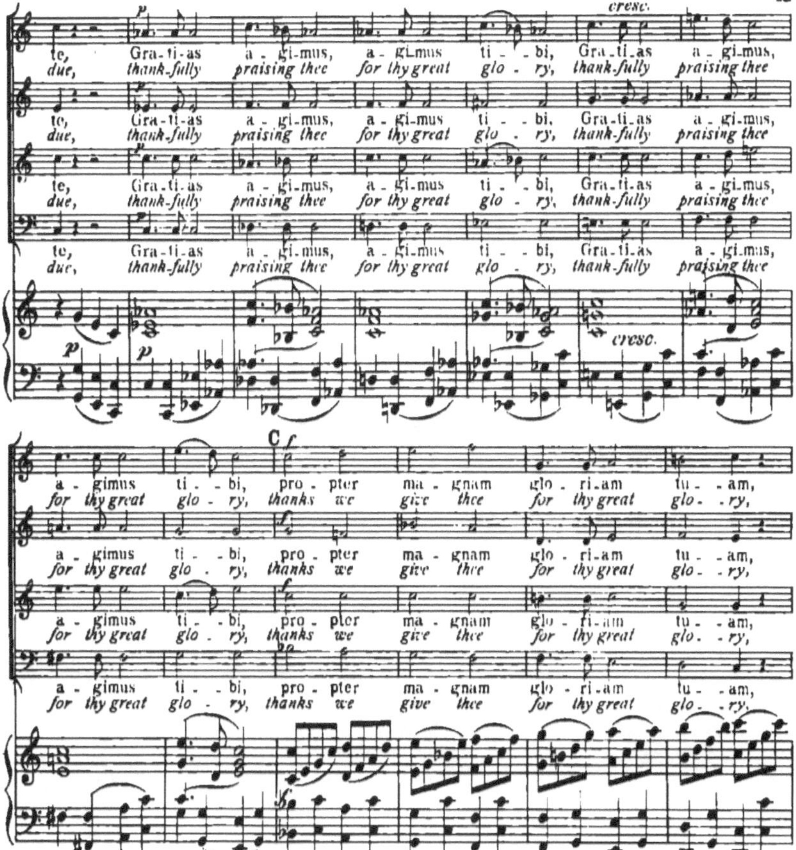
cresc.
te, Gra-ti-as a-gi-mus, a-gi-mus ti-bi, Gra-ti-as a-gi-mus,
due, thank-fully praising thee for thy great glo-ry, thank-fully praising thee
p
cresc.
C f
a-gimus ti-bi, pro-pter ma-gnam glo-ri-am tu-am,
for thy great glo-ry, thanks we give thee for thy great glo-ry,

E

Nº 3. CREDO.

tem,— ... fac-to-rem coe-li et ter-
ty,— *who heav'n and earth hath cre-a-*

tem,— ... fac-to-rem coe-li et ter-
ty,— *who heav'n and earth hath cre-a-*

tem,— ... fac-to-rem coe-li et ter-
ty,— *who heav'n and earth hath cre-a-*

tem,— ... fac-to-rem coe-li et ter-
ty,— *who heav'n and earth hath cre-a-*

rae- ... vi-si-bi-li-um om-ni-um ___ et
ted,— *and all things that are vis-i-ble ___ and*

rae- ... vi-si-bi-li-um om-ni-um ___ et
ted,— *and all things that are vis-i-ble ___ and*

rae- ... vi-si-bi-li-um om-ni-um ___ et
ted,— *and all things that are vis-i-ble ___ and*

rae- ... vi-si-bi-li-um om-ni-um ___ et
ted,— *and all things that are vis-i-ble ___ and*

in-vi-si-bi-li-um. ___ Et in u-num
that are in-vis-i-ble. ___ And we own and

in-vi-si-bi-li-um. ___ Et in u-num
that are in-vis-i-ble. ___ And we own and

in-vi-si-bi-li-um. ___ Et in u-num
that are in-vis-i-ble. ___ And we own and

de Spi-ri-tu San - cto ex Ma-ri-a Vir - - gi - ne,
by the Ho - ly Spi - rit, in the Virgin Ma - - ry's womb.

de Spi-ri-tu San - cto ex Ma-ri-a Vir - - gi - ne,
by the Ho - ly Spi - rit, in the Virgin Ma - - ry's womb.

de Spi-ri-tu San - - cto ex Ma-ri-a Vir - - gi - ne,
by the Ho - ly Spi - rit, in the Virgin Ma - - ry's womb.

de Spi-ri-tu San - - cto ex Ma-ri-a Vir - - gi - ne,
by the Ho - ly Spi - rit, in the Virgin Ma - - ry's womb,

pp
ET HO - MO FA - CTUS EST.
And God true Man was made.

pp
ET HO - MO FA - CTUS EST.
And God true Man was made.

pp
ET HO - MO FA - CTUS EST.
And God true Man was made.

pp
ET HO - MO FA - CTUS EST.
And God true Man was made,

D

Cru - ci - suf - fered

p
Cru - ci - fi - xus,
And for our sakes
Cru - ci - suf - fered

Cru - ci - suf - fered

p
Cru - ci - fi - xus,
And for our sakes
Cru - ci - suf - fered

p

cresc.   dimin.

fi - xus   e - ti-am pro   no - bis,   e - ti-am pro
tor - ture   un - der Pon-tius   Pi - late,   on the cross was

fi - xus   e - ti-am pro   no - bis,   e - ti-am pro
tor - ture   un - der Pon-tius   Pi - late,   on the cross was

fi - xus   e - ti-am pro   no - bis,   e - ti-am pro
tor - ture   un - der Pon-tius   Pi - late,   on the cross was

fi - xus   e - ti-am pro   no - bis,   e - ti-am pro
tor - ture   un - der Pon-tius   Pi - late,   on the cross was

to,
tured,
pas-
suf-
-sus
-fered
et
and
se-
in the
-pul-
tomb
-tus
was

to,
tured,
pas-
suf-
-sus
-fered
et
and
se-
in the
-pul-
tomb
-tus
was

to,
tured,
pas-
suf-
sus
-fered
et
and
se-
in the
-pul-
tomb
-tus
was

to,
tured,
pas-
suf-
-sus
-fered
and
and
se-
in the
-pul-
tomb
-tus
was

pp

E

est,
laid.
Et
And
re-
rose
-sur-
tri-

p

est,
laid.

est,
laid.
Et
And
re-
rose
-sur-
tri-

est,
laid.

p

Ped.

88

Nᵒ 4. SANCTUS.

40

№5. BENEDICTUS.

N.º 6. AGNUS DEI.

44

no - - bis, mi - se - re - te no - - bis, mi - se - re - re
on us, have com - pas - sion on us, have com - pas - sion

no - - bis, mi - se - re - re no - - bis, mi - se - re - re
on us, have com - pas - sion on us, have com - pas - sion

no - - bis, mi - se - re - re no - - bis, mi - se - re - re
on us, have com - pas - sion on us, have com - pas - sion

no - - bis, mi - se - re - re no - - bis, mi - se - re - re
on us, have com - pas - sion on us, have com - pas - sion

dim.

no - - - - bis,
on us,

no - - - - bis,
on us,

no - - - - bis,
on us,

no - - - - bis,
on us,

dim. *cresc.*

J. C. *cresc.* *dim.* *cresc.*

50

dim.   p

do - na no - bis pa - cem, do - na no - bis, do - na
may thy peace be with us, peace be with us, peace be

do - na no - bis pa - cem, do - na no - bis, do - na
may thy peace be with us, peace be with us, peace be

do - na no - bis pa - cem, do - na no - bis, do - na
may thy peace be with us, peace be with us, peace be

do - na no - bis pa - cem, do - na no - bis, do - na
may thy peace be with us, peace be with us, peace be

D p   p cresc.

pa - cem. A - gnus De - i, do - na no - bis pa - cem. A - gnus De - i,
with us, Lamb of God, O may thy peace be with us, Hear us, O thou

pa - cem. A - gnus De - i, do - na no - bis pa - cem. A - gnus De - i,
with us, Lamb of God, O may thy peace be with us, Hear us, O thou

pa - cem. A - gnus De - i, do - na no - bis pa - cem. A - gnus De - i,
with us, Lamb of God, O may thy peace be with us, Hear us, O thou

pa - cem. A - gnus De - i, do - na no - bis pa - cem. A - gnus De - i,
with us, Lamb of God, O may thy peace be with us, Hear us, O thou

Nᵒ 7. LA COMMUNION.

Nᵒ 7. LA COMMUNION.

54 Poco più lento.

Secondo.

www.ingramcontent.com/pod-product-compliance
Lightning Source LLC
Chambersburg PA
CBHW031322280626
47169CB00019B/2615